EXPLORING BIOLOGY

ORGANISMS & ECOSYSTEMS

by
Tom Jackson

Minneapolis, Minnesota

Credits

Cover and title page, © guruXOX/Adobe Stock, © Direk Takmatcha/Adobe Stock, and © Karen Moran/Shutterstock; 3, © Anusorn Nakdee/Shutterstock; 4–5, © Andrea Chiozzi/Shutterstock; 4B, © Romolo Tavani/Shutterstock; 5T, © Hamara/Shutterstock; 5B, © lunamarina/Shutterstock; 6T, © kamomeen/Shutterstock; 6B, © Wassana Mathipikhai/Shutterstock; 6–7, © Ryszard Filipowicz/Shutterstock, and © photomaster/Shutterstock; 7T, © fizkes/iStock, © Crystal Alba/Shutterstock, © Ajit S N/Shutterstock, and © Dennis W Donohue/Shutterstock; 7B, © Public Domain/Wikimedia Commons; 8T, © Kletr/Shutterstock; 8B, © Howard University/Wikimedia Commons; 8–9, © Amehime/Shutterstock; 9T, © Jacek Chabraszewski/Shutterstock; 10T, © White Space Illustrations/Shutterstock; 10B, © Public Domain/Wikimedia Commons; 10–11, © Drazen Zigic/iStock; 11T, © Alila Medical Media/Shutterstock; 11B, © OlgaReukova/Shutterstock; 12T, © 3d_man/Shutterstock; 12B, © Dr. Norbert Lange/Shutterstock; 12–13, © Lebendkulturen.de/Shutterstock; 13T, © Morphart Creation/Shutterstock; 14T, © Hanahstocks/Shutterstock; 14B, © Public Domain/Wikimedia Commons; 14–15, © Ivanova Ksenia/Shutterstock; 15T, © Kuttelvaserova Stuchelova/Shutterstock; 16T, © Vojce/Shutterstock; 16B, © Public Domain/Wikimedia Commons; 16–17, © blue-sea.cz/Shutterstock; 17T, © Marko Blagoevic/Shutterstock; 18T, © mar_chm1982/Shutterstock; 18B, © Hugh Lansdown/Shutterstock; 18–19, © Prathankarnpap/Shutterstock; 19B, © Bearport Publishing; 20T, © DedeDian/Shutterstock; 20B, © Public Domain/Wikimedia Commons; 20–21, © Norjipin Saidi/Shutterstock; 21T, © Tennessee Witney/Shutterstock; 22T, © Passakorn Shinark/Shutterstock; 22B, © Evgeny Atamanenko/Shutterstock; 22–23, © ON-Photography Germany/Shutterstock; 23T, © chanus/Shutterstock; 23B, © Public Domain/Wikimedia Commons; 24T, © Triff/Shutterstock; 24B, © Public Domain/Wikimedia Commons; 24–25, © Tunatura/Shutterstock; 25T, © Anne Coatesy/Shutterstock; 26T, © DiBtv/Shutterstock; 26–27, © Visual Storyteller/Shutterstock; 27T, © Iri_sha/Shutterstock; 27B, © Public Domain/Wikimedia Commons; 28T, © VectorMine/Shutterstock; 28B, © Laura PI/Shutterstock; 28–29, © CoreRock/Shutterstock; 29B, © Public Domain/Wikimedia Commons; 30T, © Fotokostic/Shutterstock; 30–31, © Designua/Shutterstock; 31M, © Merkushev Vasiliy/Shutterstock; 31B, © Bruno Comby/Wikimedia Commons; 32T, © G. Lukac/Shutterstock; 32B, © vladsilver/Shutterstock; 32–33, © Ali A Suliman/Shutterstock; 33B, © Augustus Binu/Wikimedia Commons; 34T, © All Canada Photos/Alamy Stock Photo; 34B, © Kingkongphoto & www.celebrity-photos.com/Wikimedia Commons; 34–35, © Teo Tarras/Shutterstock; 35T, © Creative Travel Projects/Shutterstock; 36T, © ErebourMountain/Shutterstock; 36B, © Doug Perrine/Alamy Stock Photo; 36–37, © NaturePicsFilms/Shutterstock; 37B, © Public Domain/Wikimedia Commons; 38T, © MVolodymyr/Shutterstock; 38B, © frank60/Shutterstock; 38–39, © BIOSPHOTO/Alamy Stock Photo; 39T, © Daniela.cardenas.v/Wikimedia Commons; 40T, © J. Marini/Shutterstock; 40B, © Jpedreira/Wikimedia Commons; 40–41, © Jaswe/Shutterstock; 41B, © J. Marini/Shutterstock; 42–43, © PeopleImages/iStock; 42T, © Don Landwehrle/Shutterstock; 42B, © Public Domain/Wikimedia; 43B, © Gabriele Maltinti/Shutterstock; 44B, © Creative Travel Projects/Shutterstock; 45T, © Ali A Suliman/Shutterstock; 45B, © BIOSPHOTO/Alamy Stock Photo; 47, © Teo Tarras/Shutterstock.

Bearport Publishing Company Product Development Team

Publisher: Jen Jenson; Director of Product Development: Spencer Brinker; Editorial Director: Allison Juda; Editor: Cole Nelson; Editor: Tiana Tran; Production Editor: Naomi Reich; Art Director: Kim Jones; Designer: Kayla Eggert; Designer: Steve Scheluchin; Production Specialist: Owen Hamlin

Statement on Usage of Generative Artificial Intelligence

Bearport Publishing remains committed to publishing high-quality nonfiction books. Therefore, we restrict the use of generative AI to ensure accuracy of all text and visual components pertaining to a book's subject. See BearportPublishing.com for details.

Library of Congress Cataloging-in-Publication Data is available at www.loc.gov or upon request from the publisher.

ISBN: 979-8-89577-494-6 (hardcover)
ISBN: 979-8-89577-536-3 (paperback)
ISBN: 979-8-89577-502-8 (ebook)

© 2026 Arcturus Holdings Limited.
This edition is published by arrangement with Arcturus Publishing Limited.

North American adaptations © 2026 Bearport Publishing Company. All rights reserved. No part of this publication may be reproduced in whole or in part, stored in any retrieval system, or transmitted in any form or by any means, electronic, mechanical, photocopying, recording, or otherwise, without written permission from the publisher. Bearport Publishing is a division of FlutterBee Education Group.

For more information, write to Bearport Publishing, 3500 American Blvd W, Suite 150, Bloomington, MN 55431.

Contents

Understanding Organisms and Ecosystems . . . 4
Classification 6
Bacteria 8
Bacterial Cells 10
Protists. 12
Plants. 14
Simple Invertebrates. 16
Arthropods. 18
Lower Vertebrates 20
Fungi 22
Ecosystems 24
Food Webs. 26
Carbon Cycle 28
Other Cycles 30
Dry Biomes 32
Wet Biomes 34
Ocean Zones 36
Symbiosis. 38
Symbiogenesis. 40
The Future of Organisms and Ecosystems. . . . 42

Review and Reflect 44
Glossary. 46
Read More 47
Learn More Online 47
Index 48

Understanding Organisms and Ecosystems

Earth is populated by millions of different species, including animals, fungi, plants, and bacteria. These living things, or organisms, come in many different shapes, sizes, and colors. Scientists believe each of these living things can be traced back to one single-celled organism that divided billions of years ago. Since then, life-forms have evolved over time to fill a diverse array of ecosystems worldwide in which living things depend on one another for survival.

Soil

Soil is composed of air, living organisms, minerals, and organic matter. Scientists estimate that more than 50 percent of all life on Earth can be found within the dirt. A single teaspoon of healthy soil can contain up to one billion microorganisms from thousands of different species.

Soil supports life on Earth by filtering water, preventing flooding, trapping carbon dioxide, and helping plants grow.

Asteroids and Comets

The planet existed long before it had organisms. Scientists think that around four billion years ago, a series of asteroids and comets slammed into Earth, making the planet's surface too hot to support living things. This theory is known as the Late Heavy Bombardment. Scientists believe the debris crashing into Earth came from the movement of other large planets.

Asteroids are rocky remnants of leftovers from the formation of the solar system. They are most often found orbiting the sun between Mars and Jupiter.

The Horseshoe Crab

Scientists estimate horseshoe crabs have been on Earth for about 450 million years. This is longer than almost any other animal species still alive today! Despite their name, horseshoe crabs aren't actually crabs—they are arthropods, which makes them more closely related to scorpions and spiders.

One horseshoe crab can lay about 4,000 eggs in a single cluster. Each year, the mother can lay about 100,000 eggs.

Classification

Scientists have identified more than one million species on Earth, and they predict that there are many millions more that have yet to be discovered. To make sense of the great variety of life, all life-forms are organized into groups using a system based on shared characteristics called classification.

Ancestors

Taxonomy is the science of identifying, describing, and classifying all life on Earth into different groups of creatures that are related to one another. All individuals of a particular group share a class or order evolved from a common ancestor who lived long ago. A small group, such as a genus, has only a few species, and their common ancestor probably lived relatively recently. A phylum is a bigger group that contains hundreds of thousands of species, and their single common ancestor lived long ago.

A type of feathered dinosaur is the ancestor of the birds around today.

Binomial System

Scientists created a binomial system to give every species a scientific name made of two words. The first word is called the generic name. It is the name of the genus the species belongs to. The second word is the specific name, which is a unique name for that species. Many of the words used in taxonomy are based on old languages, such as Latin and ancient Greek. They often describe the group in some way. For example, bats belong to an order called Chiroptera, which means hand wings. Humans belong to the *Homo sapiens* species, meaning wise human.

Taxonomy divides life into a series of groups called taxons, which go from broader to more specific. The most specific grouping is species.

The human species is part of a larger genus called *Homo*. There used to be other species in this genus, such as *Homo erectus* and *Homo neanderthalensis*, but they have died out.

The *Homo* genus belongs to a family, Hominidae, that it shares with other great apes: chimpanzees, gorillas, and orangutans.

The Hominidae family is one of several in the Primate order, which also includes monkeys, lemurs, and gibbons.

Primates are members of the Mammalia class, along with whales, lions, and mice.

Mammals are one class of the phylum Chordata, which includes anything with a backbone, such as reptiles, birds, and fish.

The animal phyla combine to make up the Animalia kingdom. There are several other kingdoms of life on Earth, which include life-forms such as plants, fungi, and bacteria.

TAXON	HUMAN	CHIMPANZEE	BLUE WHALE	SNAKE
Species	*sapiens*	*troglodytes*	*musculus*	*naja*
Genus	*Homo*	*Pan*	*Balaenoptera*	*Naja*
Family	Hominidae	Hominidae	Balaenopteridae	Elapidae
Order	Primates	Primates	Artiodactyla	Squamata
Class	Mammalia	Mammalia	Mammalia	Reptilia
Phylum	Chordata	Chordata	Chordata	Chordata
Kingdom	Animalia	Animalia	Animalia	Animalia

HALL OF FAME

Carl Linnaeus
1707–1778

The taxonomy system was originally organized by Swedish plant scientist Carl Linnaeus in 1735. Linnaeus established the same set of taxons we still use today, but he didn't understand the process of evolution. Instead, he grouped organisms according to how they looked. This led to early mistakes, such as grouping whales and dolphins as kinds of fish—though he later changed this.

DID YOU KNOW? Taxonomists have shown that the fungal kingdom is more closely related to the animal kingdom than it is to the plant kingdom.

Bacteria

Among the smallest and oldest types of life are bacteria. Fossil remains show that these microscopic organisms were living on Earth almost four billion years ago. Bacteria are far too small to see without powerful microscopes. They live in all habitats, from the depths of the ocean to the peaks of the highest mountains. Bacteria even live underground and float around in the air.

> Bacteria evolved at a time when the conditions on Earth were very extreme. Today, they can be found living in places where no other life-forms can survive, such as in hot springs.

Single Cells

A single bacterium has a body made of one cell, which measures about 2 millionths of a meter (2 μm). The cell is surrounded by a membrane and a rigid cell wall. Inside the cell, there is a complex mixture of deoxyribonucleic acid (DNA) and other chemicals of life. Most bacteria cells are spherical or rod-shaped, but a few have a twisted shape. They sometimes grow into clusters made up of several cells.

Cyanobacteria are blue-green algae that float in the ocean as plankton. It is estimated that for every human on Earth, there are three trillion cyanobacteria in the sea.

HALL OF FAME

Ruth Ella Moore
1903–1994

In 1933, Ruth Ella Moore became the first Black American woman to earn a degree in biology. She worked on the germs that caused tuberculosis—a lung disease that is still one of the biggest killers today. Moore also showed that gum disease and rotting teeth are caused by bacteria in the mouth that eat the remains of sugary foods.

The colors in water come from the microbes living there and their waste chemicals.

Good and Bad Bacteria

Some bacteria cause illness, such as an upset stomach and sore throat. They can be treated with germ-killing drugs called antibiotics. Bacteria can also infect wounds and damage the body, and so they must be cleaned away with antiseptics. However, bacteria in some foods, such as yogurts and pickles, do not cause harm. They add acids to make these foods taste the way they do. These food bacteria are even useful to the body because they help with digestion. In fact, there are billions of bacteria living inside your intestines right now!

When bacteria turn the sugars in milk into lactic acid, it makes yogurt. This gives the sharp taste and creates the gooey mixture.

Archaea are microbes found in hot springs. These small organisms look a lot like bacteria and have been around for just as long. However, archaea have a distinct metabolic system. So, they form a separate kingdom.

DID YOU KNOW? The weight of all bacteria on Earth is around 77 billion tons (70 billion t). That's 45 times heavier than all the world's animals combined!

Bacterial Cells

Bacteria have smaller and simpler cells than more complex organisms, such as animals and plants. The most obvious difference is that there is no nucleus within a bacterial cell. Instead, the cell's DNA is floating in a rough bundle. This makes the bacterial cell prokaryotic—a cell that lacks a nucleus and other organelles.

Types of Bacteria

There are two main shapes for bacterial cells. A rounded cell is called a coccus, while a rod-shaped bacterium is called a bacillus. When bacteria form into long chains, they are called streptococci or streptobacilli. Cocci bacteria also form in clusters known as staphylococci. A pair of joined round bacteria are called diplococci. Less common cell shapes are bean shapes, comma shapes, long and thin filaments, and spirals.

There are about 30 trillion cells in the human body and about the same number of bacterial cells living on your skin and in your stomach.

The names used to describe bacteria depend a lot on how the cells appear under a microscope. Another way to identify different bacteria types is to use dyes that target certain chemicals in the cell.

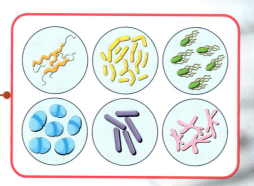

HALL OF FAME

Alice Catherine Evans
1881–1975

Alice Catherine Evans was an American expert in bacteria. She studied diseases found in milk and cheese and helped make these foods much safer. Evans also discovered which bacteria caused dangerous infections of the skin and blood in the 1940s—around the same time the first antibiotic medicines were being developed.

Cell Features

Bacteria life processes happen in the cytoplasm, which is a complex mixture of chemicals. The only obvious internal feature in bacteria is the bundle of DNA. A membrane surrounds the cell, and it may include long taillike flagellum or shorter extensions called pili. A cell wall surrounds the membrane, and in some cases the whole cell is inside a protective capsule.

DNA
Cell membrane
Pilus
Flagellum
Cytoplasm
Cell wall
Capsule

The cell wall of a bacterium is made from mostly a complex sugar-based chemical called murein.

Bacteria also helps our digestion by breaking down foods that our stomach chemicals cannot. Yogurt is full of healthy bacteria.

DID YOU KNOW? There are bacteria that eat rocks! Some are found living about 2 miles (3 km) underground, using the chemicals in the rocks for energy.

Protists

Protists are single-celled organisms that have much larger and more complicated cells than bacteria. Some biologists put all the protists into one kingdom, but they are a varied group of organisms. Protist cells have many internal structures, just like the cells of multicellular life-forms. Some protists live like animals, plants, or both at the same time!

Flagellates and Ciliates

A large group of protists get their name from the flagella and tiny hairlike cilia on their cells. Flagellates are responsible for algal blooms where seawater is filled with planktons, killing off other forms of life. Ciliates are common in soils and even live as parasites inside animals. They move their cilia to pull tiny food particles to a mouthlike opening in the cell.

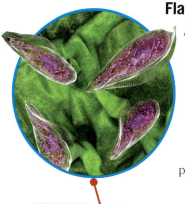

These flagellates have one flagella each, but some have two, three, or several dozen.

Some animallike protists are called amoebas. The cell of an amoeba has no rigid walls, allowing it to squirm into any shape. Many amoebas are parasites that live inside animal bodies and cause diseases.

Diatoms

Diatoms are plantlike protists that live in seawater, lakes, rivers, and sometimes damp soil. They use photosynthesis to make food from sunlight. Diatoms are either rounded or boat-shaped, and their cells sit inside a shell-like case made from silica, which is the same chemical found in sand.

A diatom's case is in two halves. The lower half always fits snugly inside the upper one.

HALL OF FAME

Antonie van Leeuwenhoek
1632–1723

The first person to see protists was Antonie van Leeuwenhoek. In the 1670s, he made improved versions of the microscope and soon discovered a hidden world of microscopic life. He called the organisms animalcules, meaning little animals. He described many types that we now recognize as ciliates, amoebas, and other kinds of protists.

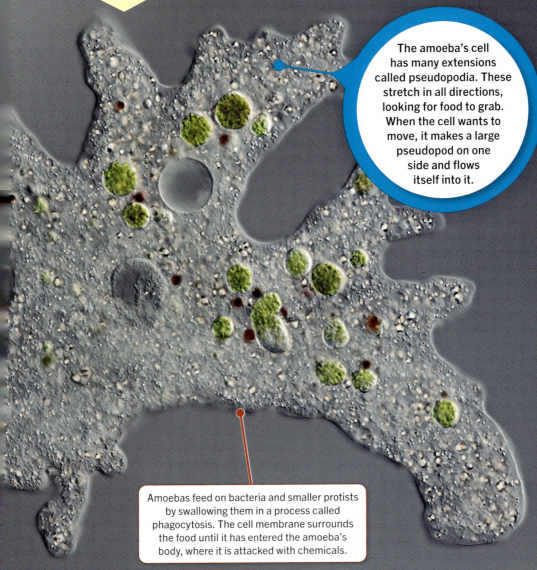

The amoeba's cell has many extensions called pseudopodia. These stretch in all directions, looking for food to grab. When the cell wants to move, it makes a large pseudopod on one side and flows itself into it.

Amoebas feed on bacteria and smaller protists by swallowing them in a process called phagocytosis. The cell membrane surrounds the food until it has entered the amoeba's body, where it is attacked with chemicals.

DID YOU KNOW? A protist called *Plasmodium* causes the deadly disease malaria that kills around 600,000 people each year. A new vaccine is being tested to stop it.

13

Plants

There are around a quarter of a million species of plants that make up the kingdom Plantae, with members ranging from tiny mosses to towering trees. Plants power their bodies through photosynthesis—a process that uses the energy in sunlight to make sugar from water and carbon dioxide. Aside from the coldest and driest habitats, plants are found in all parts of the world.

The giant sequoia is one of the largest and longest-living organisms on Earth. It grows to about 280 feet (85 m) tall and lives for more than 3,000 years!

Internal Vessels

Moss is one of the simplest kinds of plants. It grows over surfaces, and its flat body has no distinct roots, stem, or leaves. Mosses are nonvascular plants, which means they don't have a channel to transport water or nutrients. Vascular plants, such as ferns, conifers, and flowering plants, have vessels that can transport water and sugar around them. This makes their bodies stiff enough to grow up toward the light.

The giant sequoia is a conifer. It uses cones to breed and make seeds. Most plants grow flowers, not cones, for this purpose.

Moss is mostly green because it is full of a green chemical called chlorophyll that absorbs red and blue sunlight in order to make food.

HALL OF FAME

Janaki Ammal
1897–1984

Janaki Ammal was one of the first women to study botany. She bred new kinds of crops that would grow better in her home country, India. This allowed the country to produce more of its own food. At the same time, Ammal also campaigned to keep as many of India's natural habitats as possible.

Seaweed

Seaweeds are plants that live in the oceans. They are not usually included in the Plantae kingdom. Instead, seaweeds are types of algae that grow into large, multicellular bodies. They photosynthesize and need sunlight to survive as land plants do, and so they grow mostly in shallow, sunlit water. Seaweeds have no roots but are anchored to the seabed. Instead of leaves, they have fronds that float in the water.

When the tide goes out, seaweeds are exposed to the air. Many seaweeds cover their fronds in waterproof slime to stay moist.

Trees usually grow above smaller plants to collect more sunlight. They strengthen their bodies with wood to grow tall.

DID YOU KNOW? Plants make up 80 percent of all the living material on Earth! In total, that is 496 billion tn. (450 billion t).

Simple Invertebrates

Invertebrates are animals with no backbone or hard skeleton inside their body. They make up around 97 percent of all animals. Invertebrates come in a great variety of shapes and sizes. The simplest of all are sponges, which form funnel-shaped bodies for filtering food from water. Other invertebrates include worms, jellyfish, and mollusks.

A sea slug is a kind of mollusk that has no shell. Other mollusks without shells include squids and octopuses.

Soft Bodies

Jellyfish belong to the phylum Cnidaria. These water-dwelling creatures are all soft-bodied animals with tentacles that have stinger cells capable of shooting poison darts into anything that touches them. In addition to jellyfish, this phylum includes corals and sea anemones. Unlike most animals, cnidarians do not have a head. Instead, their bodies are rounded with a mouth in the middle.

The fried egg jellyfish swims by squeezing its bell-shaped body, which pumps out jets of water.

HALL OF FAME

Hope Black
1919–2018

Hope Black was an Australian expert on mollusks. As a teenager, she started work at the National Museum of Victoria. Within 10 years, Black became the first woman to be made a national curator in Australia. In 1959, she joined one of the first female teams to explore Australia's Antarctic islands.

Mollusks

Mollusks form a large group of invertebrates. Many mollusks, such as snails and slugs, live on land, but most of them are aquatic animals. They often protect their bodies with shells. Snails have a single shell, while shellfish, such as clams and oysters, have two shells connected by a hinge.

A mollusk's shell is made mostly from a hard stonelike chemical called calcium carbonate. This shell protects the animal's body and keeps it moist.

A sea slug has bilateral body symmetry, meaning the right and left halves of its body are mirror images. There is a head at one end where the mouth, brain, and main sense organs are located. The other end has a rear opening for waste.

The antennae on the head of a sea slug are rhinophores that are used for detecting chemicals in the water.

DID YOU KNOW? The geography cone shell is one of the most venomous animals in the world. Its venom is 10 times more powerful than a king cobra's!

Arthropods

The largest animal phylum is the invertebrate group Arthropoda. Its phylum name means jointed foot, referring to how these animals have an armorlike exoskeleton, or hard outer skeleton, made up of interlocking jointed sections. An arthropod's exoskeleton is made from a flexible plastic-like material called chitin. There are three main subgroups in this category: insects, arachnids, and crustaceans.

Insects

Insects are by far the largest group of arthropods. In fact, 80 percent of all animal species are insects. Insects have six legs and bodies in three sections, with a head, thorax, and abdomen. They often have one or two pairs of wings on the thorax. It is thought that insects were the first animals to evolve flight around 320 million years ago. Common kinds of insects include beetles, flies, ants, and butterflies.

The scarab has a tough cover protecting its wings.

Crustaceans

Crustaceans have a varied number of legs, often with limb-like appendages that are used as pincers. Most of them live in the ocean. Copepods and krill—two types of crustaceans that live as plankton—are among the most numerous animals on Earth. Larger crustaceans, such as lobsters, toughen their exoskeletons with calcium carbonate. Other crustaceans include barnacles that glue themselves to rocks, filtering food from the water with their feathery legs.

Pill bugs are among the few crustaceans that live on land. However, they can survive only in moist habitats, such as among fallen leaves. Some species can roll up into a ball to fend off threats.

DID YOU KNOW? Very few kinds of insects live in the ocean, with the major notable exception being sea skaters. All others live on land or in fresh water.

Arachnids have eight legs and limb-like mouthparts called palps. Most arachnids kill using venom. The venom turns their prey to mush, which the arachnid then slurps up.

A spider has two body sections. Its legs are attached to the forward section, called the cephalothorax. The rear section is the abdomen.

Spiders create netlike webs of sticky silk to snare prey. The arachnids use their feet to pick up any vibrations from movement in their webs.

HALL OF FAME

Margaret S. Collins
1922–1996

Margaret S. Collins started attending university at the age of 14. She became only the third Black American woman to become a doctor of zoology. Collins became an expert in termites—wood-eating insects that live in huge colonies and can damage houses made from wood. She was also a leading figure in the civil rights movement in Florida.

Lower Vertebrates

> Amphibians spend the first stages of their lives in water, swimming around as fishlike tadpoles. They then grow legs, transforming into adults that move to land.

Vertebrates are animals with backbones and internal skeletons. All of today's vertebrates evolved from fish that first appeared around 500 million years ago. The first land vertebrates were amphibians—the ancestors of today's frogs and salamanders. From there, these land animals evolved into reptiles and the ancestors of mammals. Birds evolved later from dinosaurs.

Reptiles

Reptiles have skin covered in tough, waterproof scales, and—unlike fish and amphibians—they are not reliant on water to breed. There are three major types: turtles and tortoises, crocodiles, and squamates. This last group is by far the largest, containing snakes and lizards. Most reptiles lay eggs with a waterproof shell, but a few give birth to live young. They are cold-blooded, meaning their bodies are the same temperature as their surroundings.

> Snakes have evolved to slither on their bellies without legs. There are about 4,000 species, and 600 of them use venom to kill prey.

HALL OF FAME

Bertha Lutz
1894–1976

Bertha Lutz became a leading expert in poison dart frogs. These brightly colored little amphibians collect poisons from the insects that they eat and store them in their waxy skin. Even touching these frogs can cause sickness or even death for predators, so animals learned over time not to attack the frogs. Two frog species and four lizards are named after her.

Fish gills are located behind the head. Water enters the mouth, flows through the gills, and then out through slits on the side of the neck.

Fish

There are 33,000 species of fish. They live in oceans, rivers, and lakes. Fish use gills to take oxygen from the water, although a few species can breathe air for short periods. They have streamlined bodies that flow easily through the water, and they use tail fins for swimming and side fins for steering. The back, or dorsal, fin stops them from rolling onto their sides as they swim.

The horned frog of South America has a mouth that is large enough to swallow prey that is the same size as the frog!

Adult frogs have no tails, while salamanders and newts keep their tails into adulthood. Amphibians return to water to breed. Their eggs have no shells and will dry out unless they are laid on or under the water.

DID YOU KNOW? The marine iguana is the only lizard that feeds under the sea. It eats seaweed. When food is scarce, the lizard shrinks in size to save energy.

Fungi

Fungi is the third kingdom of multicellular organisms alongside plants and animals. There are 140,000 known species of fungi. The most familiar are mushrooms that sprout from the damp ground, but these are only the fruiting bodies that grow to spread the fungi's spores. The rest of the organisms are growing unseen below the ground or inside plants—and even on our bodies!

Bright colors on fungi often warn animals not to eat them. These organisms often contain dangerous poisons. Most mushrooms will make you sick, so only eat the ones sold in stores.

External Digestion

Fungi are saprophytes, which means they grow on their food. They do not have a mouth or stomach. Instead, they release digestive enzymes that break food down into a sloppy mush outside the fungus's body. Then, the fungus absorbs the useful nutrients. Fungi play an important role of driving the decay of dead material, eating it up, and recycling important nutrients into the soil.

Mold is a kind of fungus. It thrives in damp conditions, growing from microscopic spores that float in the air and land on leftover foods.

Food and Fungus

Many mushrooms are edible and can even contain minerals and vitamins. Fungi are ingredients in other foods, as well. The blue part of blue cheese is a fungus, and most bread is made with a microscopic fungus called yeast. The yeast eats the sugars in the dough, releasing carbon dioxide gas. Bubbles of this gas make the dough rise and create a soft, springy loaf.

Dried yeast is added to bread dough. Yeast is also used to make beer and wine. The alcohol in these drinks is made by the fungus.

DID YOU KNOW? The largest living thing on Earth is a honey fungus. The fungus covers an area equivalent to that of 1,665 soccer fields!

Ecosystems

Every living thing requires a place to live as well as a source of energy and nutrients. But living things cannot survive alone. They become part of ecosystems—communities of living things that rely on one another for survival. Evolution has given organisms the tools to survive in even the harshest environments.

Coral reefs are diverse ecosystems in warm, shallow ocean waters. They are sometimes described as the rainforests of the sea due to the many species found there.

Ecological Factors

The study of ecosystems is called ecology. Ecologists have found that each ecosystem has a unique collection of factors that helps or hinders the survival of its members. Biological factors come from other species living in the area. For example, some species may be a source of food, and others may pose problems, such as predation, disease, or competition for living space. An ecosystem also has nonbiological factors, such as the weather and condition of the soil.

Ecosystems often experience different seasons throughout the year, where changes in temperature, day length, and rain levels impact the wildlife.

HALL OF FAME

Eduard Suess
1831–1914

Ecosystems of different kinds fill all of Earth's living space or biosphere. The word *biosphere* was coined in 1875 by Eduard Suess. He used the term to describe the part of the planet where life can survive, from the deepest underwater landscapes to the highest altitudes. In the 1920s, his ideas were rediscovered by scientists who were trying to understand how wildlife communities work.

Corals are tiny relatives of jellyfish. They have hard shells that are left behind when the soft parts of the creatures die. Younger corals grow on these shells, slowly building a region of rocky seabed filled with life.

Hibernation

Many animals become inactive during long, cold winters. They sleep and stay inside a warm den to save energy. Food is hard to find during the winter, so the animals rely on stores of fat built up in their bodies through the warmer months. This system of resting during the winter is often called hibernation, although in true hibernation, an animal's body processes slow down. Its breathing and heart rate become very slow.

Hedgehogs roll up in a ball of leaves to make a nest for winter.

Reef corals are found in shallow, sunlit water because they have algae living inside them. The single-celled algae feed the corals with sugars made by photosynthesis.

DID YOU KNOW? It is estimated that about 25 percent of all marine species are found in coral reefs.

Food Webs

All living things need energy and nutrients. Plants get theirs by harnessing the energy in sunlight to produce fuel using photosynthesis. Animals get what they need by eating the bodies of plants or other animals. A food web is a set of connections between members of an ecosystem, based on what is eating what.

Interconnected

A food web begins with a producer, which captures a source of energy from the wider environment. In most ecosystems, the producers are plants. The producers are eaten by primary consumers. These animals are then eaten by secondary consumers.

> The top of the food web is occupied by the apex predators, such as wolves and birds of prey.

> Some whales are filter feeders. They sift out food from the water through baleen, which is a fringe of flexible plates around their mouths.

> This pod of Bryde's whales are taking gulps of seawater filled with shoals of small fish. The whales are secondary consumers in the ocean food web.

26 — **DID YOU KNOW?** A food web is also a map of how energy flows through an ecosystem, keeping the wildlife alive.

An ocean food web is based on phytoplankton, which are tiny, photosynthesizing organisms that float in the water.

Detritivores

Plants rely on a supply of nonliving chemical nutrients in the soil. These are put there by decomposers. These are life-forms that eat the waste and remains of other living things, turning them back into soil. Fungi, bacteria, and flies are common decomposers.

A fungus grows on damp, dead wood, slowly digesting it.

Rachel Carson
1907–1964

Rachel Carson introduced the public to environmental problems caused by pollution and habitat destruction. In 1962, she wrote a book called *Silent Spring*, in which she warned that the chemicals used on farmlands were killing wildlife and threatening ecosystems. If this happened, the sounds of animals, such as birds singing in the spring, would disappear. Thanks to Carson, governments and scientists began to work harder to protect the environment.

HALL OF FAME

Carbon Cycle

All life is based on carbon chemicals. Fats, sugars, proteins, and vitamins are all made up of complex chains of carbon atoms. Organisms take in and give out carbon all the time, creating a flow of carbon through the natural environment. This is called the carbon cycle.

Natural Cycle

Carbon is drawn into the food web by plants and other producers that take carbon dioxide gas out of the air or water. The producers turn the gas into sugars using photosynthesis. Animals return some of this carbon dioxide to the environment through respiration. Some of the carbon in the remains of dead organisms becomes locked away, sinking underground. Sometimes, these carbon sinks form coal and oil.

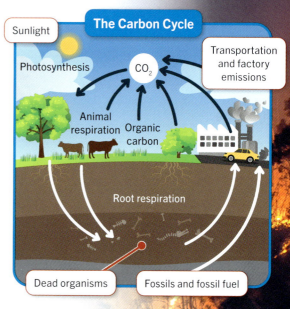

The Carbon Cycle: Sunlight, Photosynthesis, CO_2, Transportation and factory emissions, Animal respiration, Organic carbon, Root respiration, Dead organisms, Fossils and fossil fuel

Climate change is melting the world's ice and glaciers. Life-forms adapted to living in these cold places are losing their habitats.

Disrupted Cycle

In the carbon cycle, the amount taken in by life is equal to the amount given back out. However, by burning the coal, gas, and oil stored in the carbon sinks known as fossil fuels, extra carbon is added to the air. The extra carbon gases in the air trap more heat around the planet, making the world warmer and changing the climate.

DID YOU KNOW? The amount of carbon dioxide in the air today is 50 percent higher than it was in the year 1750, and it is still rising.

Climate change is making some regions warmer and drier. Forests become so dry that they burn quickly in wildfires.

It takes many decades for forests to regrow after fires. Sometimes, the areas become too dry for trees, so grasslands or deserts replace the burned forests.

Forest wood is an important store of carbon. When wildfires burn the wood, they add more carbon dioxide into the air—making climate change even worse.

HALL OF FAME

Eunice Newton Foote
1819–1888

The climate changes caused by disruption to Earth's carbon cycle were first identified by Eunice Newton Foote. In the 1840s, Foote explored how different gases absorb heat from sunlight and found that carbon dioxide got the hottest. She wondered what would happen to the climate if the amount of carbon dioxide in the air went up or down. Foote's work was originally ignored because she was a woman, but her findings were rediscovered in the 1970s.

Other Cycles

Living things need a supply of several chemicals to stay alive. Phosphorus is used in DNA and fats, and nitrogen is an essential ingredient in proteins. Plants take these nutrients from the soil, and they are passed on to animals through the food web.

Most of Earth's land is higher than the oceans. Gravity causes water to flow into streams and rivers, which eventually go down to the sea.

Nitrogen Cycle

The air is 79 percent nitrogen, but this gas is very unreactive and hard for life to take in. The nitrogen cycle relies on bacteria to take the gas from the air and turn it into soil chemicals. Lightning also converts the gas into chemicals that dissolve in rain. Animal urine and droppings add nitrogen to the soil, too. Other bacteria then reverse the process, breaking down nitrogen-rich chemicals in the soil back into pure nitrogen gas.

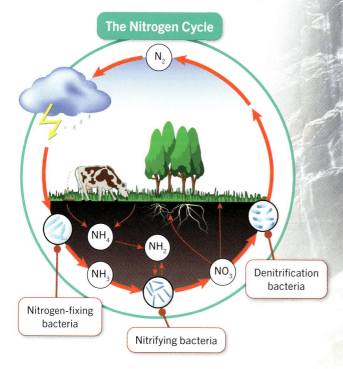

The Nitrogen Cycle

DID YOU KNOW? About 96 percent of the human body is made up of four elements: oxygen, carbon, hydrogen, and nitrogen.

Water picks up chemicals locked in the rocks and carries them downstream. Chemicals then end up in soils where they will be used by plants and other life.

The flow of water changes the landscape through a process called erosion. The water carries away rock, sand, and silt, slowly carving out river valleys.

Water Cycle

Life relies on water to survive. Most of Earth's liquid water is in the oceans and soaked into rocks deep underground. However, it is always rising up from the oceans into the air, falling down again as rain, and flowing over the land back to the sea. This is called the water cycle. It is driven by the warmth of the sun, which turns liquid water into water vapor. As this vapor cools, it turns back into liquid and falls as rain.

Although the total amount of water on Earth never changes, it is always on the move.

James Lovelock
1919–2022

James Lovelock worked as a scientist and engineer for nearly 80 years. He is most remembered for his Gaia hypothesis, which is a way of understanding how the entire planet works as a self-controlling system. Lovelock described how Earth's systems maintain stable conditions. Many of these processes take many thousands of years.

HALL OF FAME

Dry Biomes

There is a close relationship between a place's climate and the wildlife communities that survive there. The world is divided into biomes based on this. Dry biomes do not have much rainfall each year. They include deserts, grasslands, and also the polar ice sheets.

Low Rain

Deserts are areas where less than 10 inches (25 cm) of rain falls each year. Grasslands and semi-deserts get more rain, but not enough for trees and forests to grow. Low rain is sometimes caused by rain shadows, where all the moisture in the air falls as rain on one side of tall mountains. Only dry air reaches the other side. Dry lands are also found far inland where no rainclouds can reach. Large, hot deserts form in the regions on either side of the equator.

Camel humps are filled with oily fats that can provide the animals with food and water for several days.

Bison live on the North American prairies formed by the rain shadow of the Rocky Mountains.

Emperor penguins are the only animals to spend the winter in Antarctica. The males look after baby chicks during this time, while the females feed at sea.

Cold Deserts

The driest place on Earth is not the Sahara desert. It is Antarctica, where it is almost always below freezing. That means all the water here is frozen, and there is no liquid water at all. Very few plants and animals survive in the Antarctic desert because of the cold temperatures and lack of water. Most animals there live in the ocean and come on land only to rest after feeding out at sea. They get their water from their food.

32

HALL OF FAME

Vandana Shiva
Born 1952

Vandana Shiva is an Indian environmentalist campaigning for farmers across the world to return to traditional methods, especially in places where water and nutrients are scarce. Shiva suggests that this will boost harvests and help keep soils fertile. However, some say that chemical fertilizers and genetically modified crops will be a better way of growing food on the changing planet.

Camels are well adapted to a life in the dry, sandy deserts of Africa and Asia. Their wide feet spread out, so they do not sink in the sand.

Dry biomes have few plants, and the soil lacks nutrients. Instead, it is loose sand, and any rain that does fall trickles right through.

DID YOU KNOW? About 40 percent of Earth's land is covered in dry biomes that receive less than 51 in. (130 cm) of rain each year.

Wet Biomes

Land areas with high rainfall develop into forests or wetlands. All the water allows trees to take over. If the tops of the trees form a single leafy layer, the habitat is a forest. Woodlands have gaps between the trees. A wetland occurs where the rainwater cannot drain away, creating marshes or swamps.

> Rainforests and jungles grow in tropical areas close to the equator. These areas are always warm and wet, so plants can keep growing all year round.

Boreal Forest

The world's largest forests are in cool parts of the world near the poles. Nearly all of these biomes are found in the northern hemisphere, and so they are called boreal forests, since boreal means north. For most of the year, these forests are covered in snow. The trees are evergreen conifers, which grow only during the short summers.

Moose—the world's largest deer—live in boreal forests. Most other big animals live in the sea or on savannas and grasslands.

HALL OF FAME

Wangari Maathai
1940–2011

Wangari Maathai set up the Green Belt Movement, which helped people living in rural Africa—especially women—plant more trees in order to create a more fertile habitat. Tree planting restored forest areas that had been cleared for fields and created new opportunities for local communities.

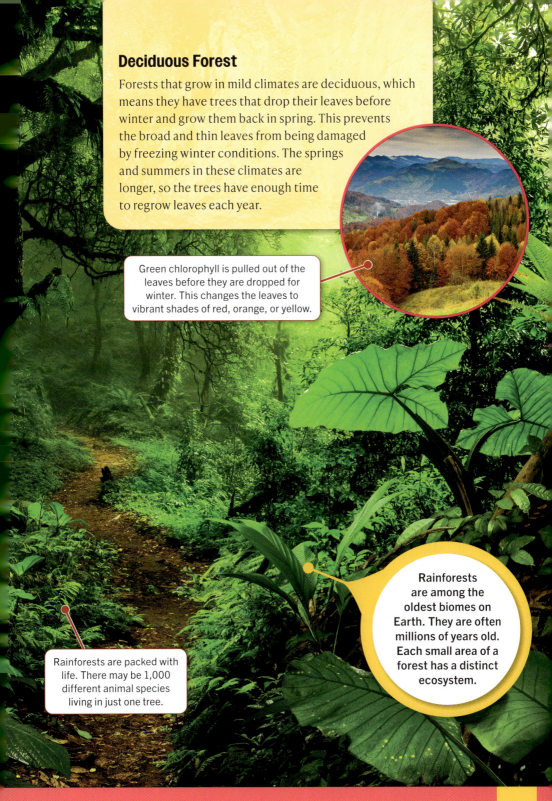

Deciduous Forest

Forests that grow in mild climates are deciduous, which means they have trees that drop their leaves before winter and grow them back in spring. This prevents the broad and thin leaves from being damaged by freezing winter conditions. The springs and summers in these climates are longer, so the trees have enough time to regrow leaves each year.

Green chlorophyll is pulled out of the leaves before they are dropped for winter. This changes the leaves to vibrant shades of red, orange, or yellow.

Rainforests are packed with life. There may be 1,000 different animal species living in just one tree.

Rainforests are among the oldest biomes on Earth. They are often millions of years old. Each small area of a forest has a distinct ecosystem.

DID YOU KNOW? A fifth of the world's forests have been cut down in the last 100 years.

35

Ocean Zones

More than two-thirds of Earth's surface is covered in oceans, with an average depth of about 3 miles (5 km). Most life in the ocean lives within 650 ft. (200 m) of the surface and within 125 miles (200 km) of a coast.

Depth Layers

The conditions for ocean life vary with depth. The top layer is the sunlit zone, where there is enough sunlight to photosynthesize. Next, is the twilight zone, which goes down to 0.62 miles (1,000 m). Many animals stay hidden in this gloom during the day and then hunt at the surface at night. Below this is the midnight zone, where it is dark 24 hours a day.

> Sardines eat floating microscopic organisms called plankton. The surface waters are filled with plankton, which are an important food source for many sea creatures.

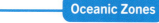

Oceanic Zones

ocean surface
SUNLIT ZONE
220 yd. (200 m)
TWILIGHT ZONE
0.6 miles (1,000 m)
MIDNIGHT ZONE
2.5 miles (4,000 m)
ABYSSAL ZONE
3.7 miles (6,000 m)
HADAL ZONE

> Plants cannot live in the deep ocean. The few animals that live down at the seabed are described as benthic.

> The hadal zone is the deepest region of the ocean only found in underwater trenches that can extend as far as 6.8 miles (11 km) below sea level.

> This angler fish has a small glowing lure dangling over its head. It gobbles up smaller fish that come to investigate the light!

In the Deep Sea

The deepest parts of the ocean are very empty, and there isn't much to eat. Some animals rely on something called marine snow, which is the constant supply of fragments of waste and dead bodies that falls down from higher up. Other animals attract prey by using bioluminescence (*bye*-oh-loo-muh-NES-unhss) to create their own light.

These fish are all trying to wriggle into the middle of the shoal, where they are safest from attack.

Sardines have mirrorlike scales that reflect back the blue of the water. This makes them harder for predators to see.

Sylvia Earle
Born 1935

Sylvia Earle is famous for her work with *National Geographic* as an explorer and educator. However, before that, Earle was a pioneer of deep-sea exploration and helped build underwater laboratories for scientists to live and work in for weeks at a time. Today, Earle is one of the Ocean Elders—a team of scientists, environmentalists, and explorers who work to protect the oceans from damage.

HALL OF FAME

DID YOU KNOW? Every year, an estimated 12 million tn. (11 million t) of plastic are dumped in the ocean. All together, this trash weighs more than 200,000 blue whales!

Symbiosis

Some organisms have evolved to live in a very close relationship with another species. This is known as symbiosis. There are three types. Mutualism is where both partners benefit from the relationship. In commensalism, one organism benefits, and the other is unaffected. Parasitism is where one species benefits at a cost to the other.

Corals have symbiotic algae living inside them. As the ocean warms, the algae leave corals, making them go white and die. This is called coral bleaching.

Lichens

The crusts that grow on rocks and bark in cold and windy parts of the world are a symbiotic partnership between a fungus and microscopic algae. The algae stay safe inside the fungus. In return, the algae feed the fungus with sugars made by photosynthesis. Other kinds of fungi buried in the soil are often in symbiosis with the plants growing at the surface.

This fungus has a hard, crusty body that stops the algae inside from drying out.

Parasite and Host

A parasite cannot live without its host, or the other living thing it is taking from. A parasite's host provides it with a place to live and a source of food. Hosts may be weakened by the exchange. Endoparasites, such as tapeworms, live inside the bodies of their hosts. Ectoparasites, such as fleas, live on the outside of the body.

A mosquito bite might deliver microscopic parasites that cause the disease malaria.

HALL OF FAME

**Meredith Blackwell
Born 1940**

Meredith Blackwell is a leading expert on parasitic fungi that take over insect bodies. The fungus grows through the body of its host—eventually killing it. Blackwell uses an electron microscope to study symbiotic and parasitic fungi.

A giant clam cannot get all the food it needs through filtering seawater alone. It has algae living in its soft body, which provide sugars in exchange for a place to live.

Giant clams always live in clear, shallow waters, where there is plenty of light for photosynthesis.

DID YOU KNOW? American badgers and coyotes are symbiotic. The coyote is able to sniff out the home of a burrowing gopher, and the badger's job is to dig it up.

Symbiogenesis

The theory of symbiogenesis is the idea that the complex cells of multicellular organisms, including humans, evolved many millions of years ago from groups of bacteria. Bacterial cells are called prokaryotic because they have cells without a nucleus or other obvious organelles. All other life, from single-celled protists to giant trees and whales, have eukaryotic cells with a nucleus and several different organelles.

Symbiogenesis is thought to have happened in a primordial soup, where simple life-forms were crowded together. This is what life was like for most of the history of Earth.

Animallike Cell

The first eukaryotic cells evolved more than 2 billion years ago. First, an archaeal cell grew larger and developed a folded cell membrane, so it had more outer surface to collect foods and nutrients. Some of the folded membrane became trapped in the cell, forming a nucleus. Next, a bacterium was eaten by the cell. However, instead of being destroyed, the incomer provided energy to the cell. It was the first mitochondrion.

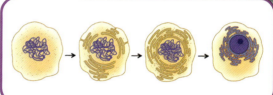

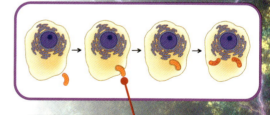

Mitochondria, shown in orange, have their own DNA that links them to a large group of bacteria that live in the oceans. A cell's mitochondria divide in two, just like bacteria.

HALL OF FAME

Lynn Margulis
1938–2011

Lynn Margulis was the leading researcher in the theory of endosymbiosis, or when one organism lives inside another. She came up with her theory in 1966 but struggled for many years to get other scientists to take it seriously. Today, endosymbiosis is accepted as the explanation of how complex life evolved on Earth.

It is thought that all the eukaryotes on Earth evolved from a single cell formed by symbiogenesis. The process may have occurred many times, but only one of these new life-forms managed to survive and reproduce.

Plantlike Cell

The first plantlike eukaryotic cells able to photosynthesize evolved some time later. Cyanobacteria, which are a kind of prokaryote, were the first organisms to photosynthesize. An animallike cell may have eaten one of these bacteria, or a bacterium may have gone inside the larger cell looking for a safe place to live. It became the first chloroplast.

A chloroplast's internal structure has many similarities with what is seen inside a free-living cyanobacterium.

DID YOU KNOW? Some of the oldest fossils of eukaryotic cells are found in rocks from India that are about 1.6 billion years old.

The Future of Organisms and Ecosystems

Around 65 percent of Earth remains unexplored. Within these unknown ecosystems, there could be millions of undiscovered species. Scientists predict that most unidentified species are single-celled organisms, such as bacteria. Some think there could be as many as one trillion species of unidentified bacteria in existence! In addition to these bacteria, scientists expect to identify many more deep-sea creatures, tropical insects, and bacteria living in extreme environments.

Climate Change

Many species may never be identified because of the climate change currently threatening organisms and ecosystems worldwide. Researchers estimate that 80 percent of Earth's land has been impacted by the problem, putting around a million species at risk of extinction. Scientists are urging people to take action before even more species and habitats are harmed.

Polar bears depend on sea ice to survive. However, the Arctic is warming even faster than the rest of the planet, causing the ice to melt.

Clearwing Moths

In 2024, a photographer visiting Guyana in South America accidentally brought home two larvae. The baby insects apparently hitched a ride on her boots! Scientists analyzed the tropical insects' DNA, discovering that they were a new species of clearwing moths, *Carmenta brachyclados*.

There are about 1,000 species of clearwing moths. The insects are sometimes called wasp moths because of their yellow-and-black coloring.

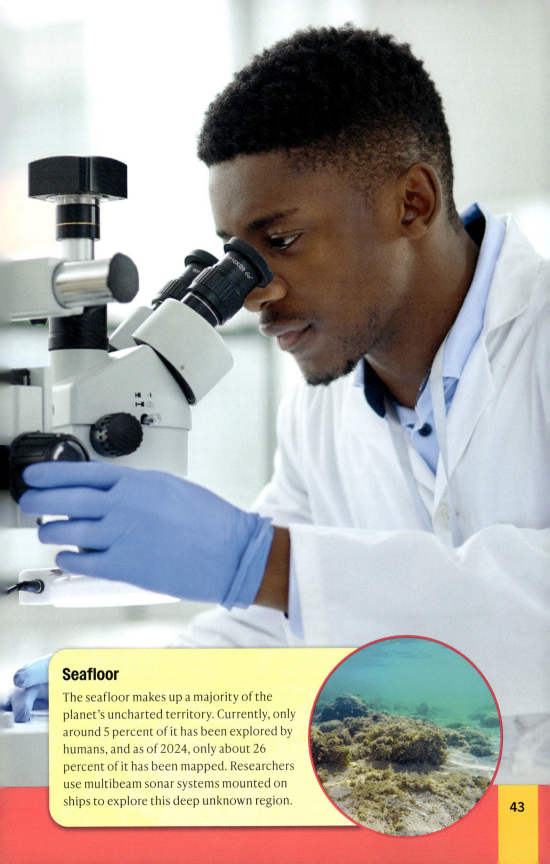

Seafloor

The seafloor makes up a majority of the planet's uncharted territory. Currently, only around 5 percent of it has been explored by humans, and as of 2024, only about 26 percent of it has been mapped. Researchers use multibeam sonar systems mounted on ships to explore this deep unknown region.

Review and Reflect

Now that you've read about organisms and ecosystems, let's review what you've learned. Use the following questions to reflect on your newfound knowledge and integrate it with what you already knew.

Check for Understanding

1. What is taxonomy? Name two groups or categories used in taxonomy. *(See pp. 6-7)*

2. How big are bacteria? Where do they live? *(See pp. 8-9)*

3. What are the two main shapes of bacteria cells? Describe them. *(See pp. 10-11)*

4. What are protists? Name and describe two types. *(See pp. 12-13)*

5. Name an example of a vascular plant and an example of a nonvascular plant. How are these types of plants different? *(See pp. 14-15)*

6. Describe an invertebrate. Name at least two invertebrates and provide a characteristic of each. *(See pp. 16-17)*

7. Which invertebrate group includes insects, arachnids, and crustaceans? In what ways are these creatures similar to and different from one another? *(See pp. 18-19)*

8. Which animals were the first vertebrates? Name three present-day vertebrates. *(See pp. 20-21)*

9. How do fungi eat their food? *(See pp. 22-23)*

10. What are ecosystems? Where do you find them? *(See pp. 24-25)*

11. What are the parts of a food web? What is the relationship among these parts? *(See pp. 26-27)*

12. Why are phosphorus and nitrogen important to living things? *(See pp. 30-31)*

13. How are boreal forests similar to deciduous forests? How are they different? *(See pp. 34-35)*

14. What makes ocean zones different from one another? *(See pp. 36-37)*

15. Name and describe the three types of symbiosis. *(See pp. 38-39)*

44

Making Connections

1. Choose two people mentioned in the Hall of Fame sidebars and name something their work has in common. How might one's work have influenced the other's?

2. How is the carbon cycle similar to the water cycle? How is it different?

3. Compare and contrast wet biomes and dry biomes.

4. In what ways are bacteria like plants? In what ways are bacteria like fungi?

5. How do you think bacteria and fungi fit into food webs?

In Your Own Words

1. Living things have changed over time. Imagine how a plant, animal, fungus, or bacterium might evolve in the future to be better suited to changed environments. Give examples.

2. If you could choose any organism or ecosystem to study, which would you choose? Why?

3. Scientists continue to learn about living things and their environments. What areas do you think they should explore further? What do you want to know more about?

4. Think about all we have learned about living things and ecosystems in the last few hundred years. How might our lives be different if we didn't know some of these things?

5. In your opinion, which person described in the Hall of Fame sidebars did the most interesting or useful work? Why do you think so?

Glossary

bacteria single-celled microorganisms, some of which cause diseases

biomes areas with certain kinds of land, climate, and living creatures

carbon dioxide a waste gas produced by the body, made of one carbon and two oxygen atoms

cell the basic unit of plants, animals, fungi, and microorganisms

chlorophyll a green chemical that plants use to help make their food

classification the arrangement of organisms into groups based on their similarities

climate the usual weather for an area over a long period of time

digestion the process of breaking down food in the body to release essential nutrients

DNA the chemical ingredient that forms genes

ecology how organisms relate to each other in their surroundings

ecosystems communities of interacting organisms and nonliving things in a habitat

eukaryotic being an organism that has cells with a nucleus and other separate structures surrounded by membranes

food web a series of plants and animals that depend on one another for food

habitats places in nature where plants and animals live

invertebrates animals without a backbone

membrane a thin, flexible layer of tissue around organs or cells

nucleus the central part of a eukaryotic cell, which controls its function and stores its DNA

nutrients substances that provide food needed for life and growth

organelles parts of a cell that do a job

organisms living things

photosynthesis the process of plants using sunlight to create sugars out of water and carbon dioxide

prokaryotic being a single-celled organism with no distinct nucleus or cell membrane, such as a bacterium or an archaeon

species a group of similar organisms that can reproduce together

vertebrate an animal with a backbone

zoology the study of animals and animal life

Read More

Kallen, Stuart A. *Climate Change Impact: Ecosystems (Climate Change Impact).* San Diego, CA: ReferencePoint Press, Inc., 2025.

Kroe, Kathryn. *What Are Fungi and Molds? (Germs and Disease).* New York: Cavendish Square Publishing, 2023.

Martin, Claudia. *Marine Ecosystems (Ocean Life).* Minneapolis: Bearport Publishing Company, 2025.

Miller, Verity. *Inside Biological Taxonomy (Inside Modern Genetics).* New York: Rosen Publishing, 2022.

Learn More Online

1. Go to **FactSurfer.com** or scan the QR code below.
2. Enter "**Organisms Ecosystems**" into the search box.
3. Click on the cover of this book to see a list of websites.

Index

algae 8, 15, 25, 38–39
amphibians 20–21
arachnids 18–19
arthropods 5, 18
bacteria 4, 7–13, 23, 27, 30, 40–42
biomes 32–35
birds 6–7, 20, 26–27
carbon dioxide 14, 22, 28–29
cell membranes 8, 11, 13, 40
chloroplasts 41
classification 6
climate change 4, 28–29, 42
consumers 26–27
coral 16, 24–25, 38
crustaceans 18
deoxyribonucleic acid (DNA) 8, 10–11, 30, 40, 42
digestion 9, 11, 22, 27
disease 8, 10, 12–13, 24, 38
ecosystems 4, 24, 26–27, 42
enzymes 22
eukaryotic cells 40–41
evolution 7, 24
fats 25, 28, 30, 32
flagella 11–12
food webs 26–28, 30
forests 24, 29, 32, 34–35
fossils 8, 28, 41
fungi 4, 7, 22–23, 27, 38–39

genus 6–7
habitats 8, 14, 18, 27–28, 34, 42
insects 18–20, 23, 39, 42
invertebrates 16–18
mammals 7, 20
microscopes 8, 10, 13, 39
mitochondria 40
mollusks 16–17
multicellular 12, 15, 22, 40
nucleus 10, 40
ocean zones 36
organelles 10, 40
oxygen 21, 30
parasites 12, 38–39
photosynthesis 12, 14–15, 25–28, 36, 38–39, 41
plankton 8, 12, 18, 36
producers 26, 28
prokaryotic cells 10, 40–41
proteins 28, 30
protists 12–13, 40
species 4–7, 14, 18, 20–22, 24–25, 35, 38, 42
symbiogenesis 40–41
symbiosis 38
vertebrates 20
vitamins 22, 28
water 4, 9, 14–18, 20–28, 30–34, 36–37, 39